Words I Know

T0100921

A Backpack Full of Verbs

by Bette Blaisdell

Content Consultant:
Terry Flaherty, PhD
Professor of English
Minnesota State University, Mankato

CAPSTONE PRESS
a capstone imprint

A+ Books are published by Capstone Press,
1710 Roe Crest Drive, North Mankato, Minnesota 56003
www.capstonepub.com

Copyright © 2014 by Capstone Press, a Capstone imprint. All rights reserved. No part of this publication may be reproduced in whole or in part, or stored in a retrieval system, or transmitted in any form or by any means, electronic, mechanical, photocopying, recording, or otherwise, without written permission of the publisher.

Library of Congress Cataloging-in-Publication Data
Cataloging-in-publication information is on file with the Library of Congress.
ISBN 978-1-4765-3936-2 (library binding)
ISBN 978-1-4765-5096-1 (paperback)
ISBN 978-1-4765-5941-4 (ebook PDF)

Editorial Credits
Jill Kalz, editor; Juliette Peters, designer; Svetlana Zhurkin, media researcher;
Kathy McColley, production specialist

Photo Credits
Shutterstock: 2xSamara, 5 (left), AKaiser, 2–3, 4–5 (back), 32, Alex Staroseltsev, 4 (top), Alexander Takiev, 15 (bottom), Anan Kaewkhammul, 14 (bottom), Andrew Burgess, cover (frog), artcphotos, 28 (bottom), Aspen Photo, 10 (right), BlueOrange Studio, 22 (bottom), Brandon Alms, 25 (top), creative, 28 (top), Dennis Donohue, 15 (top), design56, cover (backpack), Digital Genetics, 10 (left), Digital Media Pro, 21 (top), Eva Gruendemann, 9 (bottom), Gelpi JM, 13, gorillaimages, 6 (right), jordache, 23, Kafer photo, 7 (bottom), konmesa, 25 (bottom), L_amica, 19 (top), lightpoet, 9 (top), LittleMiss, 5 (top), Mandy Godbehear, 16 (bottom), 21 (bottom), Maram, 11 (top), Mihai Blanaru, 7 (top), Monkey Business Images, 4 (bottom), 17, 18 (right), mrkornflakes, 8, NatalieJean, 11 (bottom), Nelosa, 19 (bottom), njaj, 14 (top), Nuiiko, 20 (top), Odua Images, 18 (left), Peter Schwarz, 24, red-feniks, 30–31, Rick Becker-Leckrone, 27 (bottom), Ryszard Stelmachowicz, 22 (top), Samuel Borges Photography, 6 (left), spotmatik, 26 (top), Stefan Petru Andronache, 1, Stephanie Frey, 16 (top), Stuart Monk, 12, Studio 1One, 20 (bottom), Suzanne Tucker, 27 (top), tammykayphoto, 26 (bottom), wavebreakmedia, 19 (middle), Wollertz, 29

Note to Parents, Teachers, and Librarians
This Words I Know book uses full color photographs and a nonfiction format to introduce the concept of language and parts of speech. *A Backpack Full of Verbs* is designed to be read aloud to a pre-reader or to be read independently by an early reader. Photographs help listeners and early readers understand the text and concepts discussed. The book encourages further learning by including the following sections: Table of Contents, Read More, and Internet Sites. Early readers may need assistance using these features.

Printed in the United States of America in Stevens Point, Wisconsin.
092013 007773WZS14

Table of Contents

What's a Verb? 4
On the Dance Floor 6
What's Cooking? 8
This, Not That 10
Take a Look 12
Animal Talk 14
Move It 16
Class Time 18
Recess 20
Today's Weather 22
Into the Wild 24
Batter Up 26
Taking Flight 28
Like a Diamond 30

Read More 32
Internet Sites 32

What's a Verb?

What would happen
if we didn't have verbs?

Nothing.

A rabbit couldn't *jump*.
A clock couldn't *tick*.
You couldn't *laugh* or *cheer*.

A **verb** is one part of speech. It shows what people or things do or what they are.

Jump, *tick*, *laugh*, and *cheer* are words that show what something does. They're called **action verbs**.

Being verbs connect, or link, the subject of a sentence with facts about it. Marco *is* on the team. I *am* funny. Being verbs are also called **linking verbs**.

What verbs do you carry in *your* backpack?

On the Dance Floor

Have you learned a brand-new dance?
Or are there ants inside your pants?

waltz
frolic
polka
prance
two-step
foxtrot
belly dance

What's Cooking?

Cooking in the kitchen, so much to do!
I'm getting hungry. How about you?

pinch measure peel

stir
cut
chop
dice

boil
fry
poach
rinse
sautee
bake
steam
mince

This, Not That

Opposites are as different as can be.
How many opposites do you see?

add/subtract
float/sink
push/pull
stare/
blink

Take a Look

See that mirror on the wall?
Your face can smile, but that's not all!

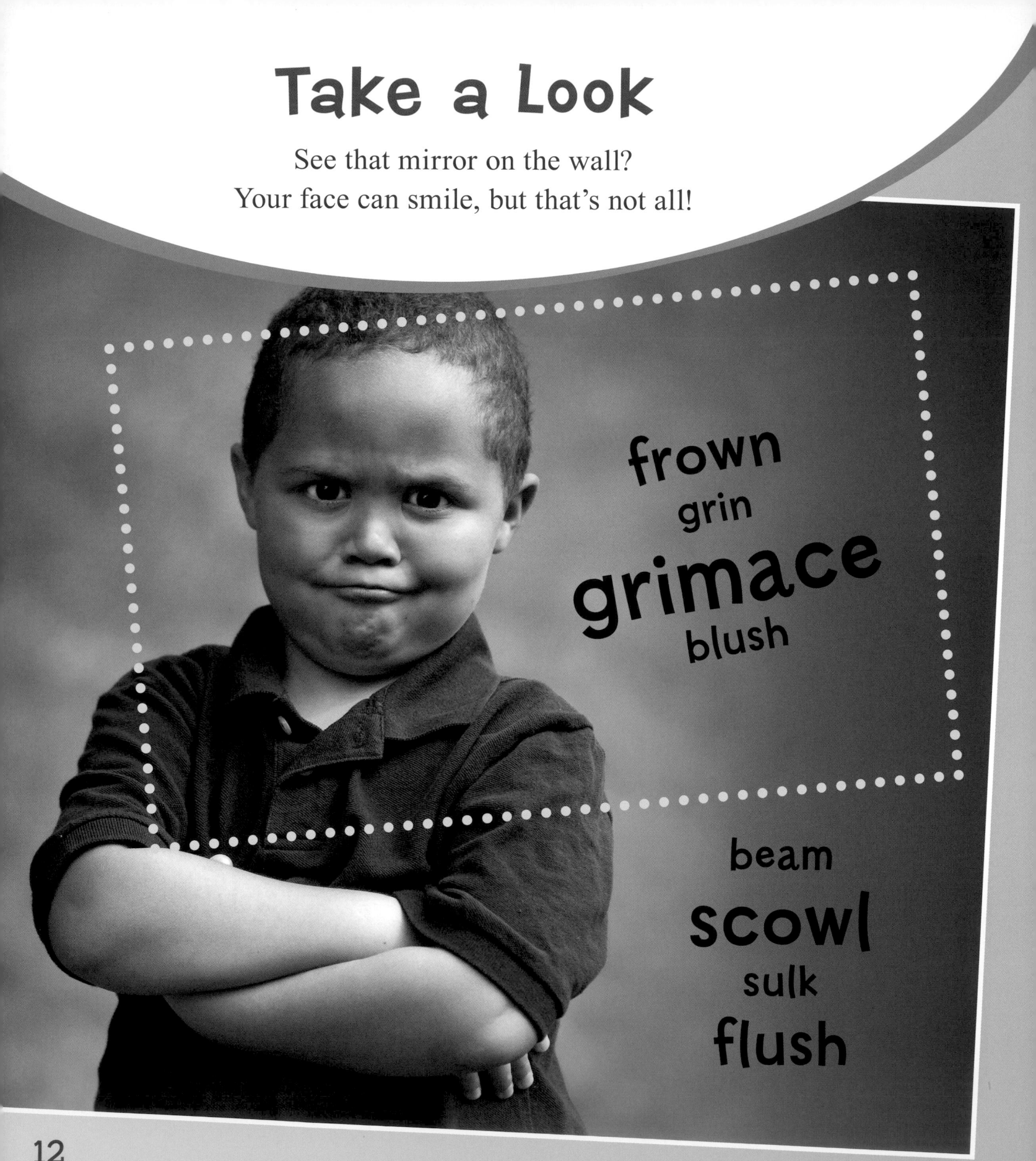

smirk
sneer
giggle
quiver
pucker
pout
laugh
shiver

Animal Talk

Did you hear a crazy sound?
Was that a moose? A mouse? A hound?

oink
bark
buzz
moo

squeak
hiss
whistle
coo

quack
squeal
trumpet
growl
gurgle
chirp
roar
howl

Move It

You could just walk, but here's a dare:
How else can you get from here to there?

slink
sneak
shuffle
clomp

sprint
gallop
hop
stomp

skip
lumber
mosey
stride
tip-toe
limp
stroll
glide

Class Time

The bell says it's time to start.
Do you love school with all your heart?

listen
group
divide
erase
9x5=45
multiply
and
punctuate

Recess

Everyone needs a little break.
Get out, get loose, wriggle, and shake!

climb
bounce
bat
slide

tumble
tag
share
hide

kick
dunk
topple
vault
toss
race
somersault

Today's Weather

Will the sun shine? Will a rainbow glow?
Peek out your door, and you will know!

rain
hail
sprinkle
drizzle

mist
rumble
thunder
mizzle

freeze
gust
swelter
snow
flood
sleet
bluster
blow

Into the Wild

How animals move is cool, it's true.
They slither and creep and fly. Can you?

stampede
flutter
dive
wiggle
crawl
scurry
stalk
jiggle

Batter Up

Grab your gear, and pick your teams.
Sports make any day better, it seems.

sweat
swing
lob
bunt

serve
score
snap
punt

Taking Flight

Of course they fly. That we know.
But can birds laugh or do-si-do?

peck
preen
squawk
roost

crow
flock
strut
hoot

migrate
nest
honk
twitter
wade
warble
screech
flitter

Like a Diamond

Late at night the stars say, "Hi!"
When morning comes they say, "Good-bye!"

flash
blaze
radiate
glint
gleam
illuminate

Read More

Fandel, Jennifer. *What Is a Verb?* Parts of Speech. North Mankato, Minn.: Capstone Press, 2013.

Ganeri, Anita. *Action Words: Verbs.* Getting to Grips with Grammar. Chicago: Heinemann Library, 2012.

Riggs, Kate. *Verbs.* Grammar Basics. Mankato, Minn.: Creative Education, 2013.

Internet Sites

FactHound offers a safe, fun way to find Internet sites related to this book. All of the sites on FactHound have been researched by our staff.

Here's all you do:

Visit *www.facthound.com*

Type in this code: 9781476539362